Introduction to Our KS1 Study Books

The central aim of Coordination Group Publications is to produce
top quality teaching and learning material which is carefully
matched to the National Curriculum, and then
supply it as cheaply as possible.

This brilliant KS1 Maths Study Book has *Three Top Features*:

Carefully Matched to the KS1 Programme of Study

*Underneath the humour and chatty style we
always make sure that our books
exactly match the requirements of the National Curriculum.
They precisely correspond with the Programme of Study and attainment targets
for KS1 Maths, levels 1-3.*

Deliberate Use of Humour

*We like to include loads of funny bits and pictures instead of giving kids
boring lists of facts to learn. The jokes are there to keep kids reading and
to keep them alert for learning the important bits.*

They're Top Dollar Value

*These study books have everything. They contain all the information
needed, they're printed in fabulous full colour, they've got loads of little
jolly bits in to tickle your humour buds — and they're a fabulous price.
That's top dollar value alright.*

Buy our books — they're ace

Contents

Section Three — Times and Divide

Section Four — Shapes and Measure

Published by Coordination Group Publications
Typesetting and layout by The Mathematics Coordination Group
Additional Illustrations by Lex Ward

Co-edited by:
Tim Wakeling BA (Hons) and Glenn Rogers Bsc (Hons)

Co-ordinated by:
June Hall BSc (Hons) PhD

Written and illustrated by:
Ruso Bradley   MSc PhD
Simon Little   BA (Hons)
Mark Haslam Bsc (Hons)
June Hall BSc (Hons) PhD
Chris Oates   BSc (Hons)
Glenn Rogers   BSc (Hons)
Claire Thompson   BSc
Tim Wakeling   BA (Hons)

Numbers 1 to 20

The Top Ten

Learn all these numbers.

1   One
2   Two
3   Three
4   Four
5   Five
6   Six
7   Seven
8   Eight
9   Nine
10   Ten

The Best of the Rest

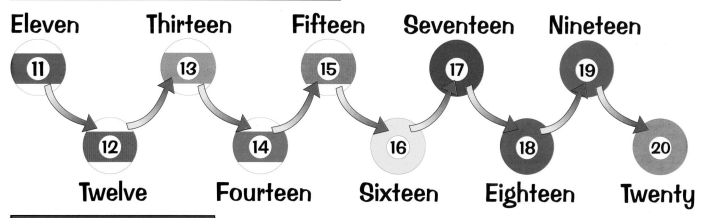

Eleven   Thirteen   Fifteen   Seventeen   Nineteen

Twelve   Fourteen   Sixteen   Eighteen   Twenty

On the Ball...

See if you can say the numbers from 1 to 20 without looking at this page. Then try to do it backwards.

How Many?

Cross them off as you Count them

Put a <u>cross</u> on each thing as you count it.
That way you won't miss any.

EXAMPLE: How many tennis balls are there in the picture?

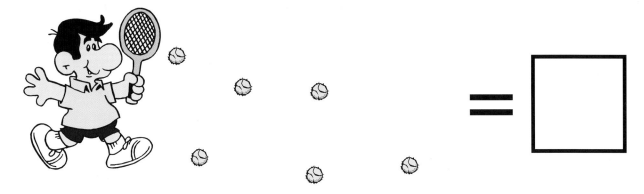

$= \boxed{}$

ANSWER: Just <u>cross them off</u> as you go.

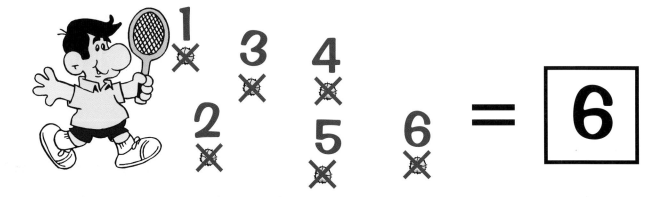

$= \boxed{6}$

Happy Birthday, dear mouse...

How many candles on the cake?

Place Value

All Numbers are Made of Digits

A <u>digit</u> is just one of these:

0 1 2 3 4 5 6 7 8 9

Put digits <u>together</u> to write bigger numbers, like <u>32</u> or <u>164</u>.

2-Digit Numbers have Tens and Ones

The <u>first</u> digit tells you how many <u>tens</u>.
The <u>second</u> digit tells you how many <u>ones</u>.

EXAMPLE: Look at the number 23

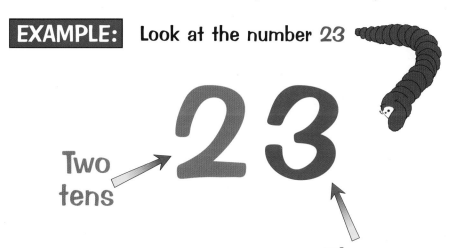

Two tens

Three ones

23 is made up of <u>2 lots of ten</u> and <u>3 ones</u>.

Try thinking of 10p and 1p coins.
23p is made up of 2 tens and 3 ones.

Bigger Numbers also have Hundreds

If there are <u>3 digits</u>, the <u>first</u> one is the <u>hundreds</u>.
The other 2 make a 2 digit number.

EXAMPLE: 127 is just <u>1 lot of one hundred</u> and <u>twenty-seven</u> more — one hundred and twenty-seven.

Money, money, money...

There is a 3-digit number on most car number plates.
See if you can spot one with a 2 in the tens bit.

Writing Numbers as Words

One-Digit Numbers

You can write numbers in <u>words</u> or <u>figures</u>.

1 One   6 Six
2 Two   7 Seven
3 Three   8 Eight
4 Four   9 Nine
5 Five

There is Zero, as well.
It's the same as nought.
You write it like this: O.

What do you get if you dial 375687264458754654684?

A sore finger.

Two-Digit Numbers

1) Write down the <u>tens</u> bit in words.
2) Then write down the <u>ones</u>.

EXAMPLE: Write 27 in words.

Write the tens bit first and then the ones bit — so it's "twenty-seven".

Three-Digit Numbers

1) First write down the number of <u>hundreds</u>.
2) Then write down the <u>tens</u> bit.
3) Lastly, write down the <u>ones</u>.

EXAMPLE: Write 127 in words.

Write the number of hundreds, then "and", then the tens and units like this:

"One hundred and twenty-seven".

(Always say "hundred" not "hundreds".)

What about writing words as numbers...

There are loads of ways to practise writing numbers. Try opening a book on any page, then write down the page number in words.

First, Second and Third

The Winner Comes First

If you've ever been in a <u>race</u>, or played a <u>game</u>, then you probably know about first, second and third already.

First   Second   Third

It's the ones <u>after</u> 3rd place that get a <u>bit</u> confusing.
Make sure you know all these:

4th (fourth)
5th (fifth)
6th (sixth)
7th (seventh)
8th (eighth)

Twenty-somethings

It may seem like the higher you go the harder it gets, but it's not true — they're dead easy.

Twenty-first
Twenty-second
Twenty-third

The <u>twenty-somethings</u> are just like the small numbers but with "twenty" on the front

21st
22nd
23rd

The same is true for the <u>thirty-somethings</u>, forty-somethings, fifty-somethings <u>and beyond</u>.

6

More, Less or the Same?

When you have two groups of something, you might need to know which group has more in it.

It's a question of Turnips

EXAMPLE: Are there more sunburnt turnips or purple turnips?

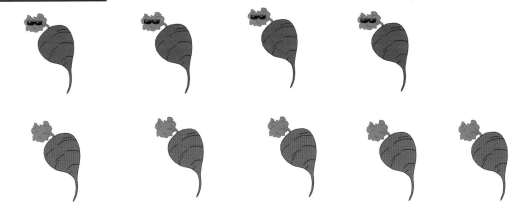

ANSWER: Just pair them up and see which is left over.

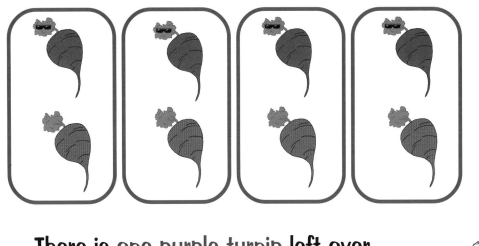

There is one purple turnip left over.
That means that there were more purple turnips to start with.

Buzz, buzz...

Are there more orange winged bees or blue winged bees?

Number Lines

The <u>number line</u> is really useful for understanding numbers.

The Number Line is Very Long

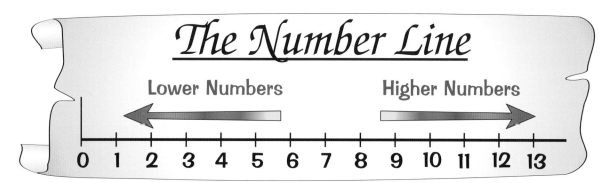

The number line is a <u>very long line</u> (in fact it goes on forever, but the page isn't quite wide enough).

Bigger Numbers are on the Right

The number line has <u>every number</u> on it, in the right order.
The further <u>right</u> you go, the <u>higher</u> the numbers get.
The further <u>left</u>, the <u>lower</u> the numbers.

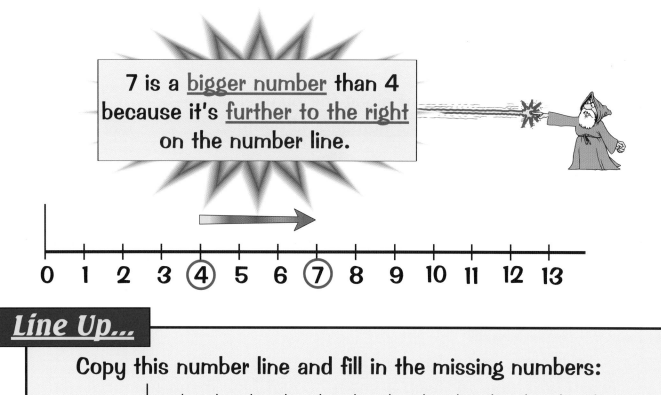

7 is a <u>bigger number</u> than 4 because it's <u>further to the right</u> on the number line.

Line Up...

Copy this number line and fill in the missing numbers:

0   1   3   4   7   8   12   13

Number Squares

Snakes and Ladders

If you've ever played <u>snakes and ladders</u> then
you'll recognise the <u>number square</u>.

Watch out for
those snakes.

EXAMPLE: <u>How many</u> numbers would you move up if
you climbed up the ladder <u>from 8 to 20</u>?

<u>ANSWER:</u>

Just count along the number line —
it's <u>12 numbers altogether</u>.

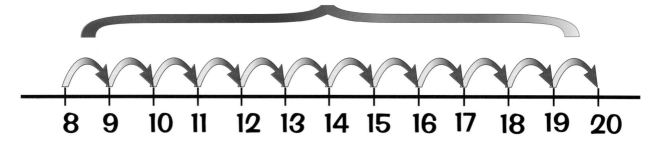

Fang-tastic...

Have a game of snakes and ladders.
Every time you go down a snake, count how many numbers you go
back. Count how many you go forward when you go up a ladder.

Putting Numbers in Order

Putting Numbers in Order of Size

If you've got a load of numbers which all have the <u>same amount</u> of digits, you can put them in <u>order</u> like this:

I want to put 72, 39, 41 and 78 in order.

This one has the <u>smallest</u> first digit, so it goes first.

3 is smaller than 4 or 7

...and 4 is smaller than 7.

41 has the <u>next smallest</u> first digit, so it's next.

Argh! We're left with 72 and 78, and they have the <u>same</u> first digit! But it's OK, 72 has a <u>smaller second digit</u>, so it goes next. That leaves 78 to be last.

That's got that question done.

So my answer is 39, 41, 72, 78.

And that's all you do — pick the <u>smallest</u>, write it down, pick out the <u>smallest</u> of the <u>rest</u>, write it down, and keep going until you've written them <u>all</u> down.

EXAMPLE: Put these numbers in order, with the smallest first:
34, 67, 25, 32.

<u>ANSWER:</u> 1) Check the digit on the left:

2) Then the next one along: 34, 32

4 is bigger than 2, so swap the numbers around.

smallest ⟶ largest

25, 34, 32, 67.

Same digit – so look at the next digit to the right.

3) So the correct order is: 25, 32, 34, 67.

DON'T FORGET:
You can only do this when <u>all</u> the numbers have the <u>same number</u> of digits.

Follow these Orders...

Put these numbers in order, with the smallest first:
13, 45, 31, 32

Combining Sets

The easiest way to <u>add</u> two lots of anything is just to <u>count</u> them.

Adding Two Sets of Things

Cross each picture off as you <u>count</u> it.

EXAMPLE: How many sheep?

ANSWER: Just <u>count</u> them — putting a cross on each one as you go.

Here you <u>added</u> 2 sheep <u>to</u> 1 sheep to get <u>3 sheep</u>.
Try adding <u>1</u> sheep to <u>2</u> sheep — you should still get <u>3 sheep</u>.

Count Down...

How many elephants?

One More, Two More

Adding <u>two more</u> is the same as adding one more,
then adding one more <u>again</u>.

Draw with a *Sharp Pencil*

For <u>drawing</u> you'll need a <u>pencil</u> and a <u>rubber</u>.

EXAMPLE: Draw <u>one more</u> elephant.

<u>How many</u> are there now?

ANSWER: Draw it, then count them, just like before.

There are now <u>5</u> elephants.

Animal Magic...

Draw two more swamp monsters.

How many are there now?

12

Adding on a Number Line

To add <u>numbers</u> it's easiest to use a <u>number line</u>.

Adding

1) Start from the first number.
2) Count to the <u>RIGHT</u> (→) along the number line.

Work out <u>4 + 3</u> using a number line.

Look at <u>page 7</u> if you don't know about the <u>number line</u>.

All you do is draw a number line and then <u>COUNT ALONG</u> it to get to the answer:

<u>ANSWER:</u>

Start at 4

Count **3** places right

1 2 3 4 5 6 7 8 9 10 11 12 13

So the answer is <u>7</u>.

You could have <u>started</u> at **3** and <u>added</u> 4 — it's just the same.

Number Line Practice...

A ruler has a number line on it.
See if you can find any other number lines.

SECTION TWO — PLUS AND MINUS

Adding Numbers Less than 10

The addition square gives you the answers to small sums.

The Addition Square

EXAMPLE: Work out 4 + 5.

Just find 4 on one side and 5 on the other.
Draw two red lines — where they meet is the answer.

Here's the 5

	1	2	3	4	5	6	7	8	9	10
1	2	3	4	5	6	7	8	9	10	11
2	3	4	5	6	7	8	9	10	11	12
3	4	5	6	7	8	9	10	11	12	13
4	5	6	7	8	9	10	11	12	13	14
5	6	7	8	9	10	11	12	13	14	15
6	7	8	9	10	11	12	13	14	15	16
7	8	9	10	11	12	13	14	15	16	17
8	9	10	11	12	13	14	15	16	17	18
9	10	11	12	13	14	15	16	17	18	19
10	11	12	13	14	15	16	17	18	19	20

Here's the 4

I'm good at addition, I'm an adder.

The red lines meet at 9, so 4 + 5 = 9

I've 'ADD enough...

What answer would get if you used the other 4 and 5?
Try it and see.

Addition Sums that make 20

There are lots of ways to make 20.
See if you can <u>learn</u> them all.

Pairs of Numbers _that make 20_

Start with an easy one:

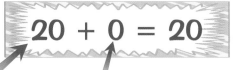

$$20 + 0 = 20$$

Take 20 and then add nothing to it.

You are left with what you started with, 20.

To get the <u>next</u> pair take away 1
from the 20 <u>and</u> add 1 to the 0.

$$19 + 1 = 20$$

The rest of the <u>pairs</u> work
in the same way — take
away 1 and <u>then</u> add 1.

$$18 + 2 = 20$$
$$17 + 3 = 20$$
$$16 + 4 = 20$$
$$15 + 5 = 20$$
$$14 + 6 = 20$$
$$13 + 7 = 20$$
$$12 + 8 = 20$$
$$11 + 9 = 20$$
$$10 + 10 = 20$$

Well, I think you get the idea...
The rest are just the same but backwards: 9 + 11, 8 + 12 ...

New Sums from Old

If you <u>know</u> the answer to one sum, you can sometimes <u>use it</u> to find the answer to a <u>different</u> sum.

And for my <u>first trick...</u>

A MAGIC TRICK

Start with an easy sum:

$$3 + 6 = 9$$

Check that it's right.
I'm now going to turn this into a new sum that is <u>still</u> right.

Hey Presto, by the power of zero
(just stick a zero on the end of every number in the sum):

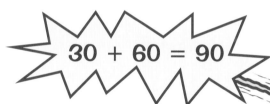

$$30 + 60 = 90$$

Spell Book

For Adding and Taking away

1) Find a sum

2) Stick a zero on every number.

3) Magic - new sum

<u>DON'T</u> use the spell book for times and divide — it is <u>only</u> for adding and taking away.

This will do the Trick...

Change this small sum into a bigger sum, by following the spell book: $4 + 7 = 11$

One Less, Two Less

This page is all about <u>taking away</u> — taking 2 away is <u>just like</u> taking 1 away <u>twice</u>.

The *World-Famous Aubergine* Question

Count the aubergines. If <u>2</u> are eaten, <u>how many</u> are left?

<u>ANSWER:</u>

Well, there are <u>5</u> aubergines to start with.
Check it yourself.
Now, put a cross on the 2 that have been eaten.

Now count the ones without crosses. I can count <u>3</u> of them — so <u>3 is the answer</u>

SLUG this out...

How many thirsty slugs are there?

If one of them has a drink and wanders off to watch TV, how many thirsty slugs are left?

Counting Back Along a Number Line

You can use the number line to find one less — or two less or...

Subtracting along a Number Line

Subtracting
1) Start from the first number.
2) Count LEFT (←) along the number line.

It's just like adding on the number line — so have a look at Page 17.

EXAMPLE: Work out 9 – 3 using a number line.

All you do is draw a number line and then COUNT BACK along it to get to the answer:

ANSWER:

Start at 9

Count 3 places left

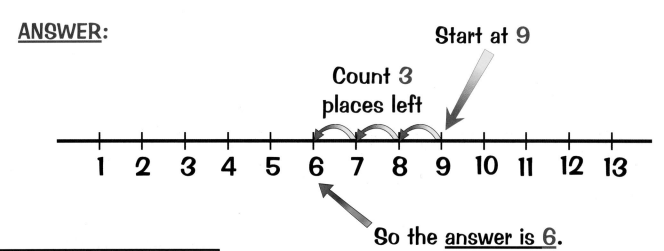

1 2 3 4 5 6 7 8 9 10 11 12 13

So the answer is 6.

Take it away...

Draw your own number line for numbers 1 to 10.
Use arrows to show 8 – 2. What is the answer?
Now take 2 from the answer. What do you get?

Differences

If you're asked to find the <u>difference</u> just take one lot <u>away</u> from the other.

Difference in _Height_

EXAMPLE: Write down the difference in height
between these two piles of bricks.

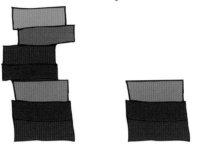

<u>ANSWER:</u> First draw a line level with the small pile of bricks.

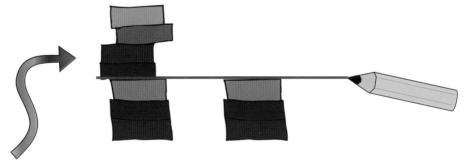

Next, count the number of bricks above the line in the big pile.
There are 4 of them so the difference in height is <u>4 bricks</u>.

Differences and _Numbers_

If you are ever asked to find the <u>difference</u> between
2 numbers, you just need to do a bit of <u>taking away</u>.

EXAMPLE: What is the difference between 5 and 2?

<u>ANSWER:</u> Well, $5 - 2 = 3$, so the difference between 5 and 2 is 3.

Spot the difference...

Write down your first name and your last name.
Which name has more letters? How many more?

Numbers that Add up to 100

Pairs that Add up to 100

Lots of different numbers add up to 100.

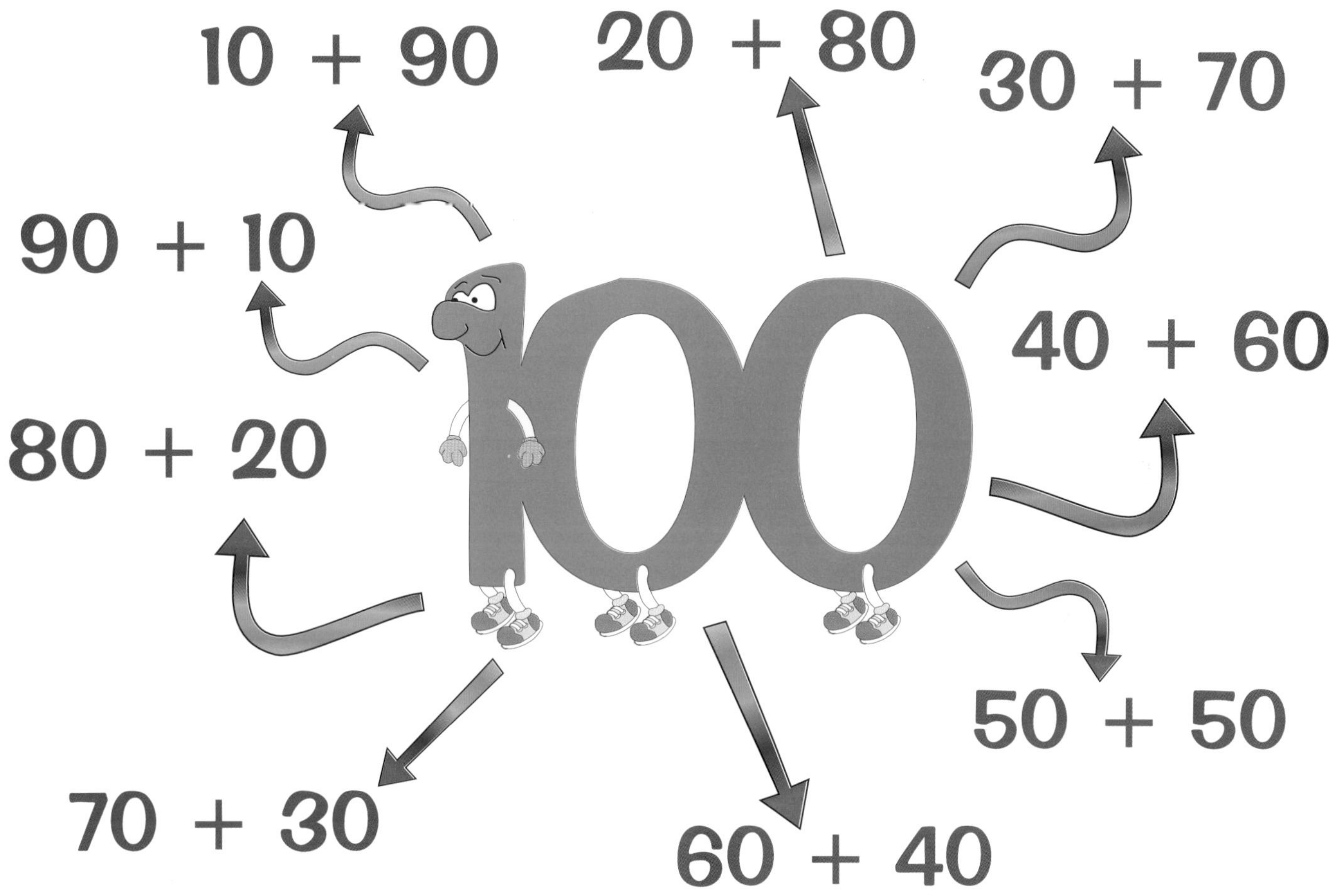

10 + 90   20 + 80   30 + 70

90 + 10

80 + 20   **100**   40 + 60

70 + 30   60 + 40   50 + 50

EXAMPLE: What number do you have to add to 45 to get 100?

ANSWER: This just means

"Find the <u>missing number</u> in 45 + ☐ = 100"

Just do 100 − 45, which is <u>55</u>.
Check that it works: 45 + 55 = 100.

Hundreds and Thousands...

A bag of crisps weighs 25 g. How much less than 100 g is this? Find something else that weighs less than 100 g. What must you add to make 100 g?

Money

Make sure you know <u>all</u> the different coins — that way you will know <u>how much</u> change you get when you buy something.

Some Coins You Should Know

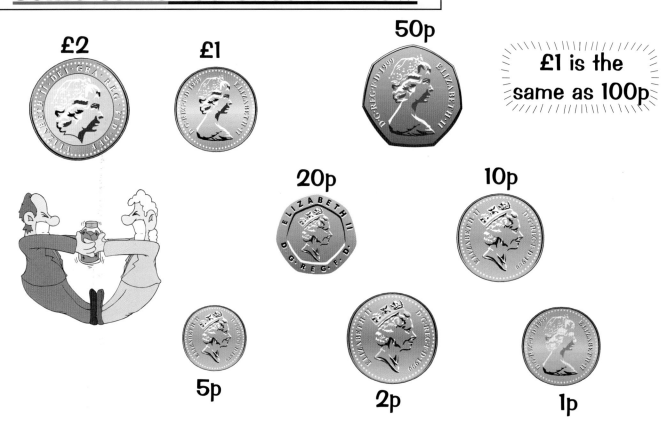

£2 £1 50p

£1 is the same as 100p

20p 10p

5p 2p 1p

EXAMPLE: In my pocket I have a 20p coin, a 2p and a 5p.
I then buy a Sherbet Surprise for 17p.
How much money do I have left?

<u>ANSWER:</u> 20p + 2p + 5p = 27p, so I started with 27p.
If I then spend 17p, I am left with <u>10p</u>.

Pocket Money...

What is the total value of these coins?

Adding and Subtracting in Your Head

Learn these tricks and amaze your friends with
the speed of your mind...

Save Time — Do Sums in Your Head

EXAMPLE Work out 35 – 12 in your head.

ANSWER:

Just split it up into 2 EASY SUMS:

Taking away 12 is
the same as taking
away 10 and then 2.

35 take away 10 is 25

25 take away 2 is 23

So 35 – 12 = 23

Boris the
whizz-pig

EXAMPLE: What is 646 + 97?

This one looks hard.
But if you do it in TWO STEPS, it's easy.

Instead of adding 97, we can add 100, then
take away 3. It works because 97 = 100 – 3.

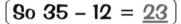

"646 + 100 is 746....

...746 – 3 is 743...

... So 646 + 97 = 743."

Use your head...

Write down 2 big addition sums and 2 big subtraction sums.
Now try and work them out in your head.

Adding Bigger Numbers

Adding Numbers

This is pretty easy stuff — I'll show you how to do it. Say I had to add up 31 and 56.

First of all, write the numbers on <u>top</u> of each other with the digits <u>lined up</u>, like this.

```
  3 1
+ 5 6
-----
```

Then add up the <u>ones column</u> (that's these bits).

```
  3 1
+ 5 6
-----
    7
```

Write the answer here.

To finish it off, <u>add up</u> this column.

```
  3 1
+ 5 6
-----
  8 7
```

That's it. So the answer's 87.

But watch out — you might get one like this tricky little sum.

EXAMPLE: Work out <u>38 + 54</u>.

Start off just the <u>same</u> — write the numbers down, above each other.

```
  3 8
+ 5 4
-----
```

But when you add up 8 and 4, you get 12.

```
  3 8
+ 5 4
-----
    2
  1
```

Put the 2 here, like before.

but put the 1 under here, in the <u>next column</u>.

and when you add up the next column, add the 1 <u>as well</u>.

```
  3 8
+ 5 4
-----
  9 2
  1
```

Keep these numbers in line...

Count up how many girls there are in your class. Now count the boys. Add these two numbers together to find how many there are in your class.

Subtracting Bigger Numbers

Subtracting is Taking Away

EXAMPLE: Work out <u>56 – 31</u>.

1)

Always put the bigger number on top.

Take away the ones first.

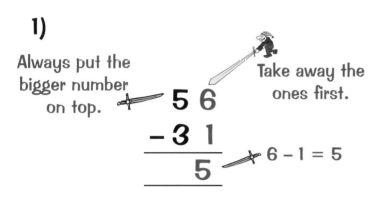

5 6
– 3 1
_____
      5

6 – 1 = 5

Subtracting Numbers

1) Write the <u>biggest number on top</u>, with the <u>ones bit lined up</u>.

2) Take away the <u>ones</u> first, then the <u>tens</u>.

Just stick to one bit at a time — <u>ones</u> first, <u>then</u> the tens.

2)

Tens next.

5 – 3 = 2

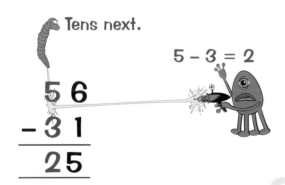

5 6
– 3 1
_____
2 5

Which means the answer is <u>25</u>.

You need to get subtraction the right way round:

68 – 55 is <u>not</u> the same as 55 – 68

...or they'll get out of control...

How many people with brown hair do you know?
How many people do you know altogether?
Now work out how many <u>don't</u> have brown hair.

Rounding Numbers

Rounding Numbers to the Nearest Ten

Rounding is just about finding the nearest number.

Three Rounding Rules

1) Draw a number line.
2) If the last digit is less than 5, the answer is the ten below.
3) If the last digit is 5 or more, the answer is the ten above.

EXAMPLE: A superhero flew into 53 windows last Thursday.
How many is 53 to the nearest ten?

ANSWER:

5<u>3</u> is between 50 and 60, but <u>3</u> is less than <u>5</u> so round <u>down</u> to <u>50</u>.

50 51 52 53 54 55 56 57 58 59 60

EXAMPLE: 15 of the windows smashed.
How many is 15 to the nearest ten?

It is in the middle if the last digit is a <u>5</u>.

ANSWER:

1<u>5</u> is exactly in the middle of 10 and 20, so round it <u>up</u> to <u>20</u>.

10 11 12 13 14 15 16 17 18 19 20

Swings and Roundabouts...

Have a look at the house numbers in your street.
See if you can round them to the nearest ten.

25

Missing Numbers

Sometimes sums have a number <u>missing</u> from the middle.

Work out what goes _in the Box_

EXAMPLE: What number goes in the box below?

$$4 + \boxed{} = 7$$

You know that 4 + 3 = 7, so the number in the box must be **3**.

EXAMPLE: Here's another one, but with a take away sum.

$$11 - \boxed{} = 6$$

Now 11 – 5 = 6, so **5** must go in the box.

Minus _is the_ Opposite _of_ Plus

To work out the number in the box, just remember that + and – are <u>opposites</u>.

EXAMPLE:

$$\boxed{} + 2 = 5$$

The opposite of <u>+2</u> is <u>–2</u>.
Now 5 – 2 = 3, so the number that goes in the box is **3**.

Some sums...

See if you can think up any more missing number sums.
How many can you think of with 20 as the answer?

SECTION TWO — PLUS AND MINUS

Picture Patterns

All you do is write the <u>differences</u> in the <u>gaps</u> between the pictures.

How Many Sprouts...

EXAMPLE: How many sprouts will be in pattern ⑤?

| ① | ② | ③ | ④ | ⑤ |

5 sprouts   8 sprouts   11 sprouts   14 sprouts   17 sprouts

+3   +3   +3   +3

ANSWER: You would need $14 + 3 = $ <u>17 sprouts</u> to draw pattern ⑤.

Write the differences here, and it's easy.

...Or How Many Worms?

①   ②   ③   ④

3 worms   5 worms   7 worms   9 worms

+2   +2   +2

ANSWER: You would need $9 + 2 = $ <u>11 worms</u> to draw pattern ⑤.

This time the difference is two.

Sprouts 'n' Worms...

1) Draw pattern ⑤ in   a) the sprout pattern
                b) the worm pattern.

Number Patterns

Number sequences are lists of numbers that follow a pattern.

Add the Same Number

JUST WRITE THE DIFFERENCES IN THE GAPS between each pair of numbers:

EXAMPLE:

1   4   7   10   13 ...

+3   +3   +3   +3   +3

The RULE is "ADD 3 TO THE NUMBER BEFORE".

The next number is 13 + 3 = 16.

To find more numbers just keep adding 3:
16 + 3 = 19
19 + 3 = 22 ...

Take Away the Same Number

I didn't mean that sort of takeaway...

EXAMPLE: Find the next term in this pattern.

20   18   16   14   12   10 ...

- 2   - 2   - 2   - 2   - 2   - 2

The RULE is "TAKE AWAY 2 FROM THE NUMBER BEFORE".

That means the next number is 10 – 2 = 8,
the one after that is 8 – 2 = 6 and so on.

Knitting Patterns...

Have a look at the house numbers on one side of a street.
What is the rule to get from one house number to the next?

Grouping 2s and 3s

It's Easier to Count Things in Groups

EXAMPLE: How many prizewinning cows does Farmer George have?

ANSWER:

There are 3 lots of 2 cows. If you count them up, there are 6 altogether. So 3 lots of 2 cows are the same as 6 cows.
You can write it out like this:

$$2 + 2 + 2 = 6$$

There's a quick way of writing this:

$$3 \times 2 = 6$$

You can say this as "three times two is six".

The fancy word for all of this times stuff is <u>multiplication</u>.

It Doesn't Matter How You Group Them

You could have said there are 2 lots of 3 cows, which is:

$$2 \times 3 = 6 \text{ cows}$$

which is exactly the <u>same</u> answer as before.

Get into Groups...

1) Draw 5 groups of 2 woolly sheep.
2) How many woolly sheep are there altogether?

Multiplication

Multiplication just means "<u>something</u>" <u>times</u> "<u>something else</u>".

The <u>Order</u> <u>of the Numbers</u> Doesn't Matter

You could count the number of "false teeth with eyes" toys by saying:

"it's <u>4</u> groups of <u>3</u>"

or <u>4</u> × <u>3</u> ...

...or "it's <u>3</u> groups of <u>4</u>"

or <u>3</u> × <u>4</u> ...

...but the answer is still <u>12</u>.

The <u>order</u> in which you multiply numbers <u>doesn't matter</u>.

Example

How many swimmers are there?

There are <u>3</u> groups of <u>2</u> swimmers,

so there are <u>3</u> × <u>2</u> = <u>6</u> swimmers altogether.

Dive into these...

1) a) Carefully copy these worms onto a big bit of paper.
   b) Divide the worms into groups of 2.
   c) How many worms are there?

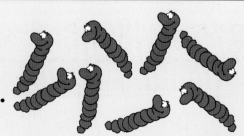

Hopping Along a Number Line

Hopping in Twos

When you <u>start with 2</u> and <u>keep on</u> adding **2**,
the numbers you get are called the <u>2 times table</u>.

1 × 2 = 2
2 × 2 = 4
3 × 2 = 6
4 × 2 = 8 ...

You can work them out using
a <u>number line</u>, like this:

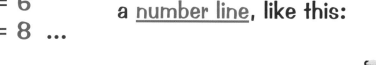

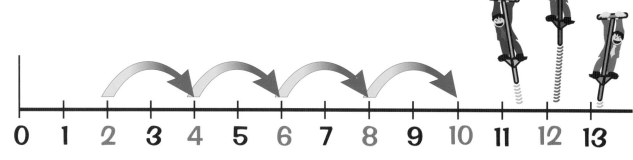

You can use the <u>number line</u> to help you with <u>any</u> of the times tables, <u>not just</u> the twos.

Hopping in Threes

If you <u>started with 3</u> and went <u>up in 3</u> each
time, you would get the <u>3 times table</u>.

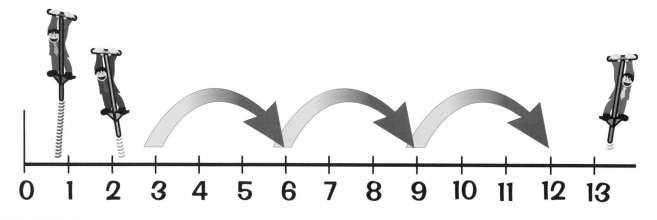

Hopping Mad...

Draw a number line up to twenty and hop along it in fours.

Times Tables

The Two Times Table is Multiplying by Two

If you <u>write down</u> what you get when you do
1×2, 2×2, 3×2, ... all the way up to 10×2,
then that's the <u>two times table</u>.

1×2=2
2×2=4
3×2=6
4×2=8
5×2=10
6×2=12
7×2=14
8×2=16
9×2=18
10×2=20

If you do 2×3 or
3×2, it's the <u>same</u>,
so you could write
it down like this:

2×1=2
2×2=4
2×3=6
2×4=8
2×5=10
2×6=12
2×7=14
2×8=16
2×9=18
2×10=20

The Ten Times Table is Easy

Here are the <u>five
times table</u> and the
<u>ten times table</u>.

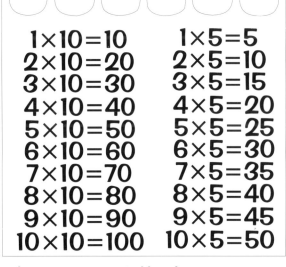

1×10=10   1×5=5
2×10=20   2×5=10
3×10=30   3×5=15
4×10=40   4×5=20
5×10=50   5×5=25
6×10=60   6×5=30
7×10=70   7×5=35
8×10=80   8×5=40
9×10=90   9×5=45
10×10=100   10×5=50

Once you know the
two and five times
tables, you <u>already
know</u> a bit of the ten
times table — 5×10
and 2×10.

I reckon the ten times tables is the <u>easiest</u> — it's like the
numbers from 1 to 10, but just with a <u>nought</u> stuck on the <u>end</u>.

Always eat your dinner at the TIMES TABLE...

See if you can learn the numbers in the 5 times table.
Then have a go at the 2 times table.

Odd and Even Numbers

All whole numbers are either even or odd.

Even Numbers

Even numbers are just the 2 times table.

2   4   6   8   are all EVEN numbers.

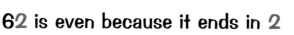

In fact, anything ending in a
0, 2, 4, 6 or 8 is an EVEN number.

EXAMPLES:

30 is even because it ends in 0

62 is even because it ends in 2

14 is even because it ends in 4

46 is even because it ends in 6

18 is even because it ends in 8

Odd Numbers

1   3   5   7   9   are all ODD numbers.

All ODD numbers end in a 1, 3, 5, 7 or 9.

EXAMPLES:

11, 83, 25, 57 and 79 are all odd numbers,
because they all end in 1, 3, 5, 7 or 9.

Odd Socks...

Have a look at the house numbers on one side of your street.
Are these numbers even or odd?
What about the ones on the other side?

The Hundred Square

Each times table makes a pattern on the hundred square.

Times Tables form a Pattern

This one is only half filled in but you can see
already that the 2s come in straight lines.

```
 1   2   3   4   5   6   7   8   9  10
11  12  13  14  15  16  17  18  19  20
21  22  23  24  25  26  27  28  29  30
31  32  33  34  35  36  37  38  39  40
41  42  43  44  45  46  47  48  49  50
51  52  53  54  55  56  57  58  59  60
61  62  63  64  65  66  67  68  69  70
71  72  73  74  75  76  77  78  79  80
81  82  83  84  85  86  87  88  89  90
91  92  93  94  95  96  97  98  99 100
```

○ 2 times table
□ 3 times table
╲ 10 times table

EXAMPLE: Find the next number in the 10 times table.

ANSWER: The 10 times table is marked off in green and makes a straight line.

To find the next number in the 10 times table, look at the next line on the hundred square:

58 59 60
68 69 70
78 79 80

Carry on the pattern, the next term is 80.

Albert Square...

1) Copy the number square, and fill in the missing circles, squares and lines in the last three rows.
2) What pattern does the 3 times table make?
3) Can you find a number that's in the 2, 3 and 10 times table?

Counting in 2s

Sometimes you can count things 2 at a time. It makes it quicker, but you need to know your 2 times table to do it.

Counting in 2s is Quicker

EXAMPLES: How many eyes do the 3 turtles have altogether?

ANSWER: This is easy if you can count in 2s.

2 4 6

So the 3 turtles have 6 eyes.

Kick Off...

How many legs do 5 runners have?

Counting in 10s

Sometimes to count really <u>quickly</u> you need to be able to do it in 10s — so you'd better make sure you <u>know</u> your <u>10 times table</u>.

Count Big Numbers in Tens

Instead of counting these gold bars one by one, you can count them in tens — easy.

10　　20　　30　　40　　50

So there are 50 gold bars.

EXAMPLES: How much money do you have if you have four 10p coins?

<u>ANSWER:</u> Just count them in 10s.

10　　20　　30　　40

So there is 40p altogether.

Did you say counting in TENTS...

1) How many coins are in 2 piles of ten?
2) What about 3 piles?
3) How many coins are here altogether?

SECTION THREE — TIMES AND DIVIDE

Doubling and Halving

If you <u>double</u> something and then <u>halve</u> it, you get back to what you started with. I'll show you what I mean...

EXAMPLE:

If you <u>double 3 strawberries</u> you get <u>6 strawberries</u>.

Now <u>halve</u> the <u>6 strawberries</u> and you'll get <u>3 strawberries</u> — which is what you started with.

EXAMPLE: What do you get if you double the size of a chocolate bar with **4** pieces?

ANSWER:

You get **4 × 2 = 8** pieces.

And if you chop the bar in <u>half</u> you get back to <u>4</u> pieces.

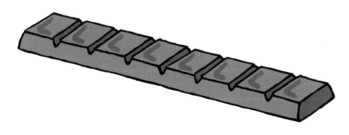  

Double Top...

Double **2** carrots and then halve them.
How many carrots do you have now?

Sharing between 2, 3 and 4

Sharing stuff is easy — everyone has to get the same...

Sharing 6 between 2

The Basic Method

1) Give them 1 each.
2) Give them another 1 each.
3) Keep going until there are none left to share.

EXAMPLE: Wendy and Kevin share 6 juicy hotdogs between them. How many do they get each?

  one each

  two each

ANSWER:

  three each

There are none left now, so that's 3 hotdogs each.

Sharing 6 between 4

EXAMPLE: Betty and Neil have turned up as well. How many is 6 juicy hotdogs shared between 4?

ANSWER:

There aren't enough hotdogs to have 2 each.
Now, if they have 1 each that's 4 hotdogs altogether, with 2 left over.

So the answer is 1 hotdog each and 2 left over.

Dividing

Division is Sharing

EXAMPLE:

Peter <u>shares</u> 4 chocolate mice equally between his two cats. Each cat gets 2 mice. We say "4 shared by 2 is 2".

In maths, they'd call this <u>division</u> or <u>dividing</u> – it sounds more impressive. But it's just <u>sharing</u>.

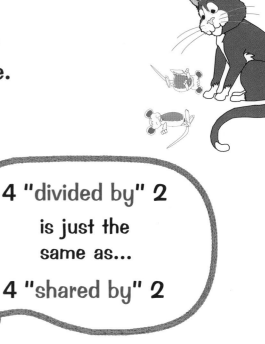

In symbols:

$$4 \div 2 = 2$$

"divided by"

4 "divided by" 2 is just the same as... 4 "shared by" 2

The Remainder is the Bit Left Over

Suppose the jar had 5 mice instead of 4. When they're shared out, each cat will still get 2, but there'll be <u>1 left over</u>. We call the bit left over the <u>remainder</u>.

What remainder was that then?

EXAMPLES:

1) 7 shared between 2 goes 3 times with remainder 1   (because $2 \times 3 = 6$)

2) 11 divided by 3 goes 3 times with remainder 2   (because $3 \times 3 = 9$)

Divide and Conquer...

1) Get 10 buttons from an adult (10 coins, 10 pebbles or 10 sweets will do).
2) Share them equally between 5 friends.
3) How many does each friend get?

Fractions

Fractions sounds like a horrible word, but it's just <u>halves</u> and <u>quarters</u>.

A <u>Half</u> is when you Split something into Two

When you cut something into two bits,
both the <u>same size</u>, you've cut it into <u>halves</u>.
Like this cucumber.

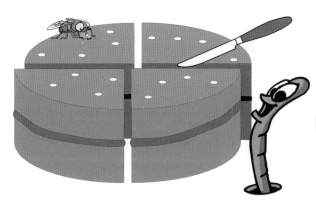

If you cut it into <u>four</u> bits that are
all the same size, it's in <u>quarters</u>.

Like this gorgeous chocolate cake.

Two <u>Quarters</u> are the Same as a <u>Half</u>

If I carefully colour in a <u>quarter</u>
of this boring square, then
colour in <u>another</u> quarter...

It's the same as if I'd
coloured in a <u>half</u>.

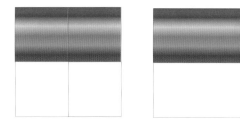

Piece of Cake...

Draw two cakes on some paper, then cut them out.
Cut one into halves and the other one into quarters.

(Even better, bake two cakes — then eat them!)

More Missing Numbers

Sums with <u>missing numbers</u> don't just have + and −.
Some have x or ÷ instead.

Work out what goes in the Box

EXAMPLE: See if you can work out what number goes in the box.

$$2 \text{ x } \boxed{} = 8$$

You know that 2 x 4 = 8, so the number in the box must be <u>4</u>.

EXAMPLE: Here's another one, but with a <u>divide</u> sum.

$$12 \div \boxed{} = 6$$

Now 12 ÷ 2 = 6, so <u>2</u> must go in the box.

You can write Number Stories to go with sums

EXAMPLE: Gerald <u>shares</u> some coconuts with his turkey, Susan. They get 3 coconuts each.

You could write it like this.

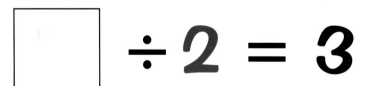

$$\boxed{} \div 2 = 3$$

Now 6 ÷ 2 = 3, so Gerald must have started with <u>6</u> coconuts.

Hard times...

See if you can think up any missing number sums, then write some funny number stories to go with them.

Missing +, –, × or ÷

It can be a bit hard if a sum has the +, –, x or ÷ missing.
But if you learn your <u>times tables</u> it's quite easy.

Write +, –, × or ÷ in the box

EXAMPLE: Here's a nice <u>easy</u> one to get started.

$$2 \;\boxed{}\; 3 = 5$$

We know that 2 + 3 = 5, so the answer is +.

EXAMPLE: Now look at this one.

$$2 \;\boxed{}\; 3 = 6$$

It looks like the first one, but be <u>careful</u> — the answer is different.
Now 2 x 3 = 6, so **X** must go in the box.

You might have to put in the = sign too

EXAMPLE: Have a look at this sum.

$$10 \;\boxed{}\; 2 \;\boxed{}\; 12$$

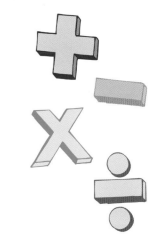

It looks hard, but the last box must be =,

so it can only be 10 + 2 = 12 .

Empty boxes...

Things like this are really easy if you know your times tables.
Try to learn your 5 times table, then think up some number
stories and sums that use it.

Estimating Numbers

Instead of counting, it's sometimes useful to make an <u>estimate</u> of an amount.

How Many?

EXAMPLE: Roughly how many green dog bones are there?

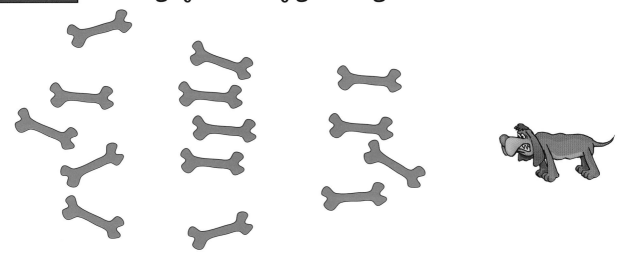

ANSWER: Instead of counting exactly, make a rough estimate.

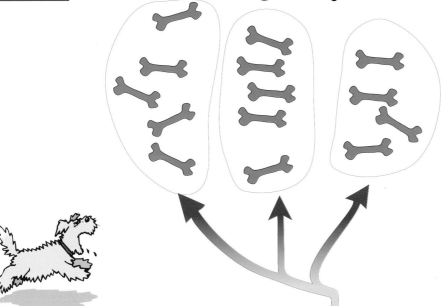

I have circled <u>3 groups of about 5 bones</u>,
so I estimate there are 3 × 5 = <u>15 bones</u>.

(Actually, if you count very carefully you'll find 14 bones)

I like ESTI, but I'm not sure about his MATE...

Estimate the number of marbles
(without counting).

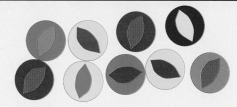

Odd One Out

If you want to be any good with shapes, you'll need to be great at spotting <u>differences</u> — so have a look at these cool pictures.

Full or Empty...

Which is the odd one out?

ANSWER:

Number 1 as he only has <u>half</u> a glass of Froggatt's Freshly Squeezed Snail Juice — the others all have full glasses.

Argh...

More or Less...

Sometimes the differences can be pretty small so you'll have to look <u>really</u> carefully.

Circle the odd one out:

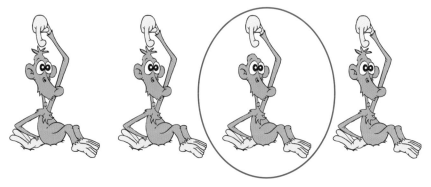

Answer: The monkey circled has no hair — the others do.

Odd Jobs...

Which man is the odd one out?

Describing with Shape Words

The words "straight" or "curved" are great for describing shapes.

Flat Shapes have Straight or Curved Edges

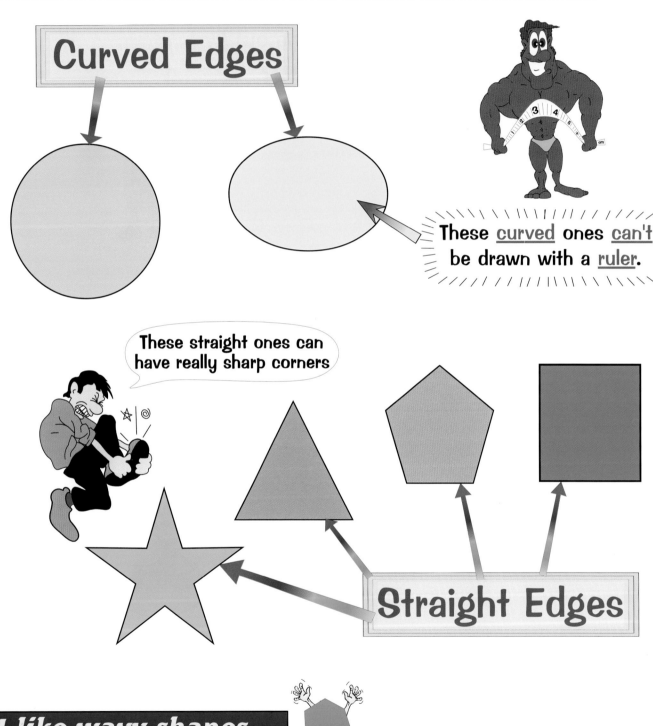

Curved Edges

These curved ones can't be drawn with a ruler.

These straight ones can have really sharp corners

Straight Edges

I like wavy shapes...

1) Make a list of 5 shapes you can see in your room.
2) Do they have curved edges or straight ones?
3) Can you see an object with both curved and straight edges?

Flat Shapes You Need to Know

Shapes with 3 or 4 sides

SQUARE

4 sides the <u>same length</u>

RECTANGLE
4 sides

TRIANGLE
3 sides

They Sometimes Look a Bit Odd

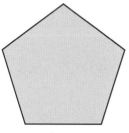

This is a <u>square</u>.
It's just turned round a bit.

This is a <u>triangle</u>.
It's got 3 sides so it has to be.

Polygons have Straight Edges

These are <u>pretty easy</u> to recognise, so long as you know <u>how many sides</u> to look for — so make sure you know them inside out.

PENTAGON
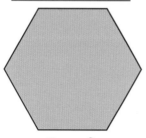
5 sides

HEXAGON
6 sides

OCTAGON

8 sides

I'm off.

Not that kind of polygon.

See how you SHAPE up...

1) How many rectangular shapes can you see in your room?
2) Can you see any triangles or hexagons?

Measuring and Estimating Lengths

That long wooden/plastic thing that sticks out of your pencil case is called a <u>ruler</u> — it is used to measure <u>lengths</u>.

Measuring Things with a Ruler

EXAMPLE: How tall is Dolly the bulldog?

<u>ANSWER:</u> All you have to do is:

Step 1) Try to stand Dolly <u>still</u> next to the ruler.
(Don't worry, she won't bite...)

Step 2) Pretend there's a line <u>from</u> the top of her head <u>towards</u> the ruler.

Step 3) Take a <u>reading</u>.
<u>70 cm</u> is the answer.

100 centimetres = 1 metre
so Dolly is <u>nearly 1 m</u> tall

I wish I'd measured this pole twice.

Always measure twice — just to be sure.

Let's see how you MEASURE up...

1) How tall is the hungry giraffe?

2) Get a friend to measure your height.
3) Are you as tall as the hungry giraffe?

Solid Shapes You Need to Know

Some are like Boxes

Cubes and cuboids have 6 faces like this one.

CUBE

Cubes and cuboids have 8 corners like this one.

CUBOID

Some have Curved Edges...

CYLINDER

The base is the flat bit that sits on the table.

SPHERE

CONE

The base of a cone is a circle.

...and Some have Triangle Faces

TRIANGULAR PRISM

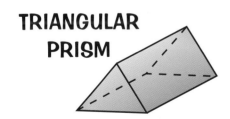

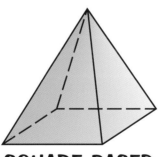

SQUARE-BASED PYRAMID

Box these up...

1) Think of an everyday object that is shaped like a sphere.
2) Can you think of any objects that are shaped like cones?
3) How many faces does a square-based pyramid have?

Big and Heavy

Scales and Measuring Jugs

Use <u>scales</u> like these
to <u>weigh</u> things.

Use a <u>measuring jug</u> to find
out how much liquid
something holds.

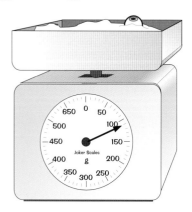

I think this
milk's gone off.

Kilograms and Litres

When you measure things, make sure you use the right <u>units</u>.
Use grams (g) or kilograms (kg) for <u>weights</u> and litres (l) or
millilitres (ml) for <u>size</u>.

**DON'T
FORGET**

1 kg = 1000 g

1 l = 1000 ml

These tell you
<u>how heavy</u>.

These tell you
<u>how big</u>.

EXAMPLES:

Milk comes in <u>pints</u> —
that's about <u>half a litre</u>.

A loaf of bread weighs
<u>800 g</u> — that's <u>nearly 1 kg.</u>

Measure up...

Write down 5 things that weigh less than 1 kg.
Now write down 5 things that hold more than 1 litre.

Time

Big Hands and Little Hands

The number the little hand is closest to tells you the hour.

Here it's just past one

Here it's nearly ten

The big hand tells you how many minutes before or after the hour.

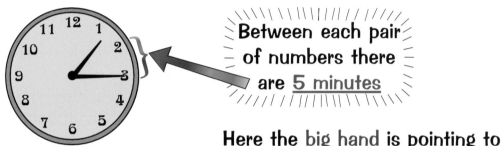

Between each pair of numbers there are 5 minutes

Here the big hand is pointing to the 3 — so that's 3 lots of 5 minutes = 15 minutes past.

Halves and Quarters

You must learn these 4 special positions for the big hand:

... o'clock   quarter past ...   half past ...   quarter to ...

EXAMPLE: "Quarter past one" is the same as "15 minutes past one".

Say What You See

To read a digital clock, just say one number after the other.

EXAMPLE: Just say "two thirty" — that's "half past two".

Days and Months

Make sure you know the <u>days</u> of the <u>week</u> and what <u>order</u> they come in — otherwise you might end up going to school at the weekend.

 Monday, Tuesday, Wednesday, Thursday, Friday, Saturday, Sunday

Days are Grouped into Months

There are <u>24 hours</u> in a day and <u>7 days</u> in a week — but the number of <u>days in a month</u> depends which month it is.

Just <u>remember</u> there are <u>12 months</u> OR <u>365 days</u> in <u>one year</u>. The weird bit is that there are 30 days in some months, 31 in others, and in February there are only 28!

There's no way out — you'll have to <u>learn</u> these:

30 days have September,
April, June and November;
All the rest have 31,
Except February alone.

<u>February</u> is the odd one out — <u>generally</u> it has 28 days but <u>sometimes</u> it has 29.

November (30 days)
December (31 days)
January (31 days)
February (28 days)
October (31 days)
March (31 days)
September (30 days)
April (30 days)
August (31 days)
May (31 days)
July (31 days)
June (30 days)

Up to Date...

1) What month comes after a) June b) January c) October?
2) Which day is between Tuesday and Thursday?
3) How many days are in a) December b) July c) a week ?

Clockwise and Anti-Clockwise

Things that <u>turn in circles</u> can do it either clockwise or anti-clockwise.

Clockwise *is Just What it Says*

If something's turning in the same direction as the clock hands then it's going <u>clockwise</u>.

Anti-Clockwise *is Just the Opposite*

If something's not going the same way as the clock hands then it's going <u>anti-clockwise</u>.

To take a lid <u>off</u> a jar you have to turn it <u>anti-clockwise</u>.

Clock these...

Draw a picture of something that is turning clockwise. Make sure you put some arrows on to show which way it's turning. Now draw a picture of something turning anti-clockwise.

Right Angles

An Angle is a Measure of Turn

What's an Angle?

The <u>angle</u> between two lines is how much you have to <u>turn</u> one of the lines so it matches up with the other one.

No, I said an <u>angle</u>.

Example

This is a half turn

Right Angles are just Quarter Turns

All the angles in squares and rectangles are right angles.

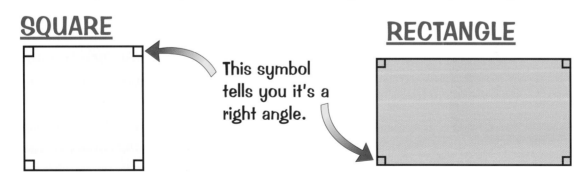

SQUARE

This symbol tells you it's a right angle.

RECTANGLE

Turn Around...

1) What fraction of a turn is a right angle?
2) Draw in a right angle symbol to show that this is a right angle:

Directions

It can be pretty tricky to explain how to get from one place to another — just <u>imagine</u> you're walking along and write down <u>every</u> turn you have to make.

Straight Lines and Turns

EXAMPLE: Describe how Bryan goes through the maze to join his friend Beryl.

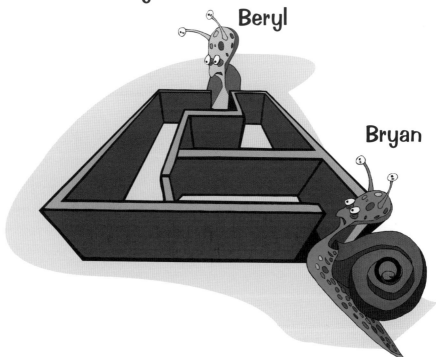

ANSWER:

1) Bryan must go forward then turn left.

2) Forward then turn right.

3) Forward then turn right again.

4) Forward then turn left and he's there.

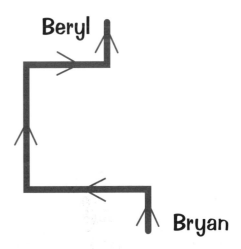

Don't get lost — learn this page...

Describe the route that Beryl would take to get to Bryan.

Mirror Symmetry

Symmetry is all about <u>changing</u> a shape so that it looks <u>exactly the same</u> on both sides of a line.

Mirror Symmetry Means Reflection

EXAMPLE:

Draw the <u>reflection</u> of the shape in the mirror line.

Mirror Line

ANSWER:

1) <u>Reflect</u> the points <u>one at a time</u>.

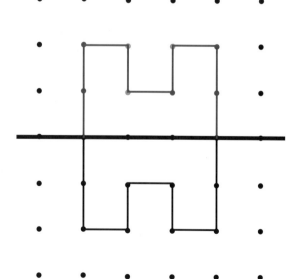

2) Count how many points are <u>between</u> the point you are reflecting and the mirror line.

3) Count the <u>same</u> number of points the other side of the mirror line and draw the <u>reflected</u> point.

4) Join up your reflected points with <u>straight</u> lines.

Mirror, mirror, on the wall...

What letter does the reflected shape make? Write down 3 other letters that you think could be made this way.

Reading Tables

Tables make things Easier to Read

This is a table.

These are tables too, but they're not quite what I had in mind...

	Simon	Kate
Favourite Food	Blancmange on toast	Gerbil flavour sawdust
Favourite Drink	Liquified cheesecake	Salted sprout juice
Favourite Sport	Unicyolo oumo wrestling	Hippopotamus tickling
Favourite Pastime	Yodelling	Underwater Cluedo

The words in the purple bits are the headings. You can use them to find out what's in the rest of the table.

EXAMPLE: What is Simon's favourite sport?

ANSWER:

1) Here's Simon.

2) Here's "Favourite Sport".

	Simon	Kate
Favourite Food	Blancmange on toast	Gerbil flavour sawdust
Favourite Drink	Liquified cheesecake	Salted sprout juice
Favourite Sport	Unicyole sumo wrestling	Hippopotamus tickling
Favourite Pastime	Yodelling	Underwater Cluedo

3) Draw lines down and across.

Drawing lines can sometimes help you find something in a table.

4) The lines cross here. So Simon's favourite sport is unicycle sumo wrestling.

Dinner Time...

Use the table to answer these questions:

1) What is Kate's favourite drink?

2) Who's favourite food is Gerbil flavour sawdust?

Bar Charts

Bar Charts show things at a Glance

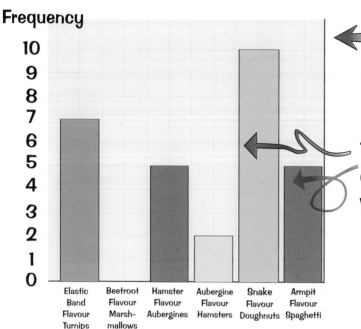

Frequency

This is a bar chart.
It shows the sales of 6 top Froggatt's products in one day from our local store.

These coloured bits going up the chart are called "bars" — that's why it's called a "bar chart".

There's no bar here — that means that no beetroot flavour marshmallows were sold. I can't think why.

The heights of the bars tell you how many of each product were sold.

EXAMPLE: According to the bar chart, how many snake flavour doughnuts were sold?

You're a snake

I'm knot!

ANSWER:
1) First look along the bottom of the chart until you find "Snake Flavour Doughnuts".

2) Now look at the bar above it.

3) What you want is the number to the left that lines up with the top of the bar. It's 10, so 10 snake flavour doughnuts were sold.

Chocolate Bars...

According to the bar chart:
1) How many Hamster Flavour Aubergines were sold?
2) How many tins of Armpit Flavour Spaghetti were sold?

Pictograms

Pictograms are even more fun than bar charts —
they have pictures instead of bars.

Pictograms *are Numbers in Pictures*

Bert went to Monsterworld for his holidays.
The pictogram shows how many times he
went on the Monster Ride each day.

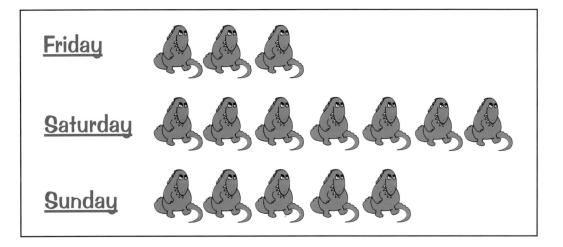

EXAMPLE: How many times did Bert go on
the Monster Ride on Sunday?

I preferred EuroDisney myself

ANSWER: All you have to do is count the pictures:

Sunday

That's 5 times.

Pretty Pictures...

According to the pictogram:
1) How many times did Bert go on the ride on Friday?
2) What about Saturday?

SECTION FOUR — SHAPES AND MEASURES

Answers

Section One Answers

Page 2   4 candles

Page 6   orange winged bees

Page 7   ├─┼─┼─┼─┼─┼─┼─┼─┼─┼─┼─┼─┼─┤
          0 1 2 3 4 5 6 7 8 9 10 11 12 13

Page 9   13, 31, 32, 45

Section Two Answers

Page 10   4 elephants

Page 11
          7 swamp monsters

Page 13   9 — The same!

Page 15   40 + 70 = 110

Page 16   6 thirsty slugs, 5 thirsty slugs

Page 17   6, 4

Page 19   75g

Page 20   85p

Page 26   1)

          2)

Section Three Answers

Page 28   1)
          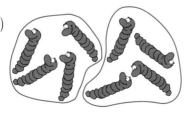

          2) 5 × 2 = 10

Page 29   1) b)

          c) 8

Page 30
          ├─┼─┼─┼─┼─┼─┼─┼─┼─┼─┼─┼─┼─┼─┼─┼─┼─┼─┼─┼─┤
          0 1 2 3 4 5 6 7 8 9 10 11 12 13 14 15 16 17 18 19 20

Page 33   1)

1	2	3	4	5	6	7	8	9	10
11	12	13	14	15	16	17	18	19	20
21	22	23	24	25	26	27	28	29	30
31	32	33	34	35	36	37	38	39	40
41	42	43	44	45	46	47	48	49	50
51	52	53	54	55	56	57	58	59	60
61	62	63	64	65	66	67	68	69	70
71	72	73	74	75	76	77	78	79	80
81	82	83	84	85	86	87	88	89	90
91	92	93	94	95	96	97	98	99	100

          ○
          □
          ╱

          2) diagonal   3) 30, 60 or 90

Page 34   10 legs

Page 35   2) 20 coins   3) 30 coins   4) 40 coins

Page 36   2 carrots

Page 38   2

Page 42   2 × 4 = 8 or 2 × 5 = 10 marbles

Section Four Answers

Page 43

Page 46   1) 8m   3) Probably not!

Page 47   1) a ball   2) Teepee/Wigwam   3) 5

Page 50   1) a) July   b) February   c) November
          2) Wednesday   3) a) 31   b) 31   c) 7

Page 52   1) quarter   b)

Page 53   Straight on, turn right, straight on, turn left, straight on, turn left, straight on, turn right and she's there.

Page 54   H.   B, C, D, E, I, O, X

Page 55   1) Salted sprout juice   2) Kate

Page 56   1) 2   2) 5

Page 57   1) 3   2) 7

Index

A

B

C

D

E

F

G

H

J

L

M

Index